I0670680

runaway clowns

Luke H. Snyder

Runaway Clowns
by Luke H. Snyder
Copyright © 2025 by Luke H. Snyder

All rights reserved.
No part of this book may be reproduced, stored in a retrieval system, or
transmitted in any form or by any means—electronic, mechanical,
photocopying, recording, or otherwise—without the prior written
permission of the author, except for brief quotations used in reviews or
scholarly works, as permitted by copyright law.

For permissions or inquiries, please contact:
Luke H. Snyder
Email: lukehenrysnyder@gmail.com

This is a work of poetry. Any resemblance to actual persons, places, or
events is purely coincidental.

Published by Banana Moon Farms
Printed in the United States of America
First Edition, August 2025

ISBN 979-8-9991150-2-7

This book was self-published through Amazon Kindle Direct Publishing
(KDP).

For

Megan Elizabeth Conversano

and

For all those who never stop speaking up
their truth
their pain
their scars

you are here
you are not crazy

you matter even when the world turns away

YOUR *VOICE IS A* REVOLUTION

We carry songs in our bodies—heartstrings pulled tight, sometimes broken, sometimes singing. We carry stories of leaving and belonging: pilgrims and refugees fleeing more than just places—fleeing silence, fear, and the expectation.

Runaway Clowns is for those who learned to hide behind painted faces, to survive in a world that demands silence and obedience, and yet still find a way to dance and resist.

These poems hold space for the lost and the found, for the masks we wear and the faces beneath—reminding us that beneath every disguise is a story worth telling, a voice worth hearing.

Luke H. Snyder

/ *runaway clowns*

the scariest goosebumps episode
wasn't the ghosts
or the haunted house

it was the one
where the girl
puts on a mask
and can't take it off

at first
she wears it for fun
but then it sticks
tight
starts changing her voice
her face
her thoughts

she forgets
what she looked like
before
she forgets
she was pretending

i think about that
every time i laugh too hard
at something that hurts
every time i smile
when i don't mean it

some of us
never take the mask off
some of us
become it

/ stuck

the small town gathered
but the parade got cancelled
no more hoe-down
someone said the clown
never showed up

but he was there
behind the trees
watching
remembering
how it felt
to be cheered
for pretending

/ *down with the clown*

do kids still run away to the circus?

climb out their bedroom windows
with a backpack and a dream
to disappear
riding boxcars
or hitching rides
past strip malls
toward
the sound of drums
and smell of hay

they should bring that back

the world was much better
when we had places
for the misfits to land —

caravan towns rolling through
with their own laws
safe harbors in the form of elephants and tents
rescuing the ones
who never fit the mold

no one asked
where you came from
only
what you could carry
and if you knew how to stay quiet
when the lion slept

some weren't running away
they were running toward
the only place
they could breathe

the world keeps closing its doors
but the circus
used to leave one open

for souls that knew
they were never meant
to stay

/ bring it back

when do children get a say?
when they're 18
shipped to a desert
to fight for oil men
who never held a rifle

mom messed up
dad too
and somehow
the kid gets the life sentence

new home
new rules
a new name maybe
just not the one
they picked

how many souls have we buried
while still breathing?

the next picasso
drawing on the back of a math test

the next tina turner
singing into coat sleeves
while the house sleeps

talent

shaking

too scared
to show the world
what it almost lost

/ *closet singers*

and while we're at it
why not let every foster kid
have their own circus

give them a home
where pretending
is finally
on their terms

we already ask them
to be someone they're not
every time
a smiling couple walks by
with checklists
and hopeful eyes

if i had to wear
a happy face
just to be picked
i'd rather be a clown

at least in the circus
they clap when you fall
and laugh when you cry

at least
they stay
long enough
for the show to end

/ auditions

i consider myself
a runaway clown too

ran so far
from who i was
i almost forgot
his name

i grew up
playing sports
when all i wanted
was the stage
the script
the spotlight

i wanted
to be strange
loud
soft
myself

but i hid
inside the bully
put on toughness
like face paint
smiled wide
so no one
would ask

i know
i hurt people
more than i can count
and for that
i'll never be
sorry enough

the tug of war
between soul and skin
between mask and mirror
left wreckage
like a tornado
through oklahoma

i wonder
where i'd be
if i hadn't started running
so young

if i hadn't been
so scared
of being seen

/ *the boy i used to be*

my son
running barefoot through the grass
laughing with his whole chest
doesn't know
his jawline
came from a man
who drank to forget
and forgot to stop
until —

his mother's laugh
carried through the walls
bright as spring light
you'd never guess
what she's held in silence

his small hands
will grow but —
bone carries memory
even when the mind forgets

i watch him
trip over a root
get up smiling

hope he drops
what we gave him
at the turnstile
and keeps walking

/ bloodline

don't give me wings yet
i just need dirt and leaves
and a small branch
to hold onto

no rush
to be beautiful

let my gut turn to liquid
in the dark
before I learn
how to fly

give me that—
slow
soft
undoing

/ caterpillar

the tax man's coming around again
even his boots
squeak to the sound
of guilt on gravel

the milkman stopped showing up
sometime after the cows were all sold
and the glass bottles
turned to plastic and shame

the repairman came
but left when he realized
he couldn't afford
his own name
stitched on a shirt
he no longer owned

now it's just me
and the porch light
waiting on someone
who doesn't ask for money
or bring bad news

maybe a clown
with a busted laugh
looking for somewhere
to disappear

/ *no more visitors*

hello my name is:
misspelled
again

new school
new friends
new lies

they ask me what i want to be
when i grow up
and i say astronaut
because i already know
how to disappear

/ *name tag*

what happens
to the jester
when the music dies?

he keeps dancing
because he knows
what will become of him
when he stops

so tell me —

is it over yet?

/ fool in the rain

change the channel —
another lie on the tv
loud —

like it knows

same thing —
these days
it's easier to believe
a conspiracy
than to admit
we're all just guessing

different haircut —
truth
disappears
while we argue
over who's right

change the channel —

same thing —

different haircut —

/ bring out the dancing monkeys

the fruit rots too quickly now
peaches bruised
before they're ripe
bananas brown
by morning
blue mold under
orange peels

i used to think
i was just slow to enjoy things
but maybe
the good stuff doesn't last
like it used to

maybe it's the weather
maybe it's the chemicals
maybe it's me

/ *ripe*

a wise friend once said
"put the needle on the record and play it, i got no place left
to hide"

music moves like river water
washes clean the heavy stones
salvation for everyone

open your ears
listen —
poets walk beside you
in the wind,
in the ordinary of this world

/ needle on the outskirts

don't wait
for the mountain to fall
to give you stones

the condor's wings stretch wide
but he won't lift your weight
climb
step by step

at the summit
clear water waits
to wash your dirty hands

/ *riprap*

i think many lost souls
met at the crossroads
on 4th street

with tattoos
and late nights

i never thanked you
for letting me bleed
for holding my wounds
and guiding me back
to my own path

but most of all
for letting me in
to your world
showing me a new way to stand

/ *cassiopeia*

another powdered wig
shakes hands —
uncle sam's wars don't all wear uniforms

some are fought in pill bottles
bathroom stalls,
and under the freeway overpass

/ untitled (3)

too many faces —
too many narratives —
which clown car is mine to follow?

/ *running from the script*

i should've listened
to the smoke you blew
talking about going south
getting away from the small town crowd

it wasn't just them —
you played against in your head
pushing me forward
so you could step back
hands clean

i should've known
from the stories i heard —
how mind games cut sharp

every day
you painted my face

turned me into bozo
for the town's eyes to laugh at
while you slipped away

/ *blue*

i am a two-headed beaver
one tries to chop the tree down
the other pulls back
the forest waits
as the river runs

/dam

like a breeze
they vanish —
no trace left

like a voice
drowned by silence —
forgotten

like the sun
dying slow —
burned out and gone

like day slipping
into night —
the mask cracks

/ *hanging by a moment*

these gentle giants
don't wear their pain like we think —
they carry the pulse of the earth

when they vanish
we lose a piece of ourselves

we wrote this ending
with smoke in the sky
and hands that don't listen

they teeter on the edge
and when they fall —
we'll follow
slow and breathless

/ ursus maritimus

i stepped into the wild
a fire burning —

i drew a map
but the path wasn't mine to keep

/proverbs 16:9

how many faces
can i wear
before the mirror
refuses to look at me

/ fairest of them all

the ghosts are back in town
not here to scare you —

just looking
for the lives
they almost had

/ *dust settles into silhouettes*

stuck between two futures —

the one
that's filled with curiosity
for technology

and the one
where my son runs barefoot
chasing birds
never asking a machine
who he is

/ *curiosity kills the cat*

these days
we set ourselves on fire
just to see
if anyone
will turn their head

/ burn the circus to get attention

it takes time
to turn inward
and bloom

yes —
we all return
to the earth

but imagine
how beautiful you'd be
if you let your colors bleed
outside the lines

just you —
finally
at rest

/ *peace inside and out*

i really thought i was okay
like finally, the noise in my head had shut up for once
but then my body
out of nowhere —
started hurting again

like it remembered something
my mind worked so hard to forget

and suddenly i was back in it
a feeling i didn't invite
in a body i didn't recognize
living a story i thought i was done telling

/ *boomerangs come back sharpened*

our souls
might be damned
but god gave us
two legs

so rejoice —
walk away

the sun still rises
over that fortress
of fables

/ *carry on*

every sign
just another stepping stone
on the way to disappearing

/ roll on down the highway

things to do in hollywood
when you're dead:

- sell your souls for headshots and auditions, yes you
  have multiple you'll find them when you're
  desperate enough
- smile for the cameras that never turn off
- wait for your name to mean something again
- let them play dress-up with your bones, like they
  still matter

we will call it —

ambition

/ *enchanté*

my face
warps in the ripple
muddy water
knows who i really am

cold creek
carries off my worry
like a leaf
it doesn't ask
where i've been

i sit
in the chill
bare
without ritual

the spirit
doesn't need
a costume
to return

/ squannacook

once a year
the wolves walk
among the sheep

no howling
no teeth
just tired eyes
stripped away from sleep

some are new
learning to smile

some are old
too stubborn to fake it

/ *town meeting*

the forest does not ask
who i used to be

i bury myself
beneath pine needles
let the rain
soften me

birds
they sing
because they are alive

barefoot
on moss and stone
i breathe

/ take a breath

burning down the highway
midnight oil in our eyes —
we swore to ride it out
to the last drop

but halfway there
we realized
no one was chasing us

so we pulled over
at the first truck stop
and bought
the cheapest bottle of wine
we could find

and that
was enough

/free will

i have endless patience
for the monsters under your bed

but forgive me
for crawling out
to feel the sunlight
on my face
every once in a while

/ *feed me seymour*

i had all kinds of friends
growing up —
plastic guys with bent arms
stuffed animals with names i forgot
a shoebox full of stars

no siblings to fight with
just long afternoons
and a loud imagination

i talked to my toys
until the words came easier
with real people

built whole cities
out of blocks and action figures
made the rules
then broke them

learned to be myself
without anyone watching

/ *imaginary friends*

if some stranger pulled up
and said
get in
i got the flux capacitor
1.21 gigawatts
and a car that can go 88 mph

i'd say —
take me to the summer
of 2009

joe corso's busted ass vacation house
in living colour reruns
cracked firewood filled with blank bullets
and alien conspiracies

we laughed too hard
jake's sister cried too long
and i still feel bad about that

but damn
it would be something
to land a flying car
right in the middle of it all

/ marty mcfly

power lines run straight to deep pockets,
                                    evergreens just fading away.

migraines keep showing up,

                    butter's gone, replaced by margarine,

cows don't roam no more.

where's my gold bowl?

gotta wash the chemicals off this fruit.

hey, can you turn your phone off?
                        it's messing with my ears.

/ *sestet #8*

no applause
no spotlight
just gravel under his boots
and a train
headed somewhere else
this is how it ends

/ *hobo*

everywhere you fly
you leave feathers behind
like ash
in the wind

some catch on barbed wire
float down creekbeds
stick in mud with boot tracks

the crow laughs from the nest he built
feathers in his beak
spirits don't forget what fed them

/ *what does that crow want?*

the crescent moon
forgot to leave
long after the morning came

maybe i will too

what if
the night
has more answers
than the day ever will

/ *wait for the return of the stars*

speaking of clowns —

humans in lab-coats wiring up plastic limbs
to fetch coffee,
mop floors,
tuck the children in
so they can sit
thinking they're not animals

microchips for every burden,
forgetting
we're still bones,
breath,
and shit

/ shortcuts

don't wave peace flags
in someone else's language
when you're too scared
to breathe their air

/ the spirit of america

fear in clean clothes
isn't wisdom

it's just a joke
worn by those
too scared to see
what real pain looks like

/ *first world problems*

don't light a fire
under a new moon
the sand will shift underfoot

you can pray
but the ocean
won't rise

/ *new moon uprising*

bound to some tree
swing creaks in the wind
back and forth
like old thoughts

/ *life is a tire swing*

no more copper coins
tossed into the wishing well
capitalism
is in our heads too

/ nickel for your thoughts

this chaos
is not new
it just finally
has our attention

/ what the fuck is going on

when did we all agree
this was normal

ordering joy
with free shipping
on our lunch breaks

replacing trees
with places to park
and calling it
growth

we traded
wonders for wifi
and never looked back

now we can't look up
from the blue light
because we don't
want to miss something

/ *choking on our convenience*

maybe this concrete jungle
is not a cage

maybe
we are just
evolving into
a different kind of wild

new animals
are always watching
from the cracks

waiting
to teach us
how to belong

/ *embrace the change*

the next ark
won't float on water

circuits sparking
in silicone skin
a thousand robots
two by two

while we
stay behind
watching the flood
we built
with our own hands

/ *noah's ark of the future*

makeup on the sink
face still smudged
in the lines you forgot to wash off

red nose, tattered shoes
flask in the side pocket
could it be any more obvious

you didn't say goodbye
slipping away down the side road

lit a cigarette
watched the ash fall
tried not to think
about balloons

nobody follows
runaway clowns

/ the circus leaves you too

the wolves
do not wait
for your excuse

and neither
does the sun

/ nature wasn't built to wait

if you keep
waiting for the right time
you'll spend
your whole life
dangling
from a thread
that never pulls

/ *jump*

the branch
grows from something older
than your fear

you have listened to its creak
long enough to know
this moment was coming

either you fall into the arms
of the wind
or you stay a shadow
clinging

sometimes freedom
sounds like breaking

sometimes
it looks like letting go
before you are ready

/ *believe in the fall*

two devils
hold a key
deep inside
a rose bush

thorns sharp

secrets?
the scent —

a promise?
a warning?

/ *the key*

the same force
that holds the sun
holds us too

yet we spin
out of rhythm

always missing
each other's light

/ re-align

they still believe
the president runs things

as if
the hands on the puppet
are hidden
behind the curtain

but i've seen
how the wolves move in silence
and how roots
undermine stone

this place
was sold long ago
to men with no names
and forests with no trees

they let him
wave at the crowd
while the pipeline
slips quietly
through sacred ground

/ *new world order*

all green is gone
as yellow settles

pollen in your throat

surrender
the bloom

/ fade away with the pollen

a bee
stuck in my lungs
when you left

buzzing
where the breath
used to be

/ black and yellow

too many stones
in this field to plant

the flood washed away
the tobacco —

i kneel in the mud
and mourn what won't return

/ *spruce pine blues*

shooting stars
they flare
with everything they have
then disappear

just like we do
when we finally
feel alive

/ just for a moment

a flower
for your body —
to rest in its own skin

a flower
for your mind —
to grow past the noise

a flower
for your spirit —
to remember you are whole

/ *offering*

inhale —
the world enters you

exhale —
you return the favor

/ ceremony

and still
i think i feel
butterfly wings
brushing past my ribs
as i turn to leave

/ *soft serve*

you can't run
from water
once your skin
has learned to drink it
like the earth
knows how to hold rain

/ *water is water if water is wet*

who will stay
when the boot heel drops
and the dirt flies
who will hold your hand
not just when the sun is warm
but when the ground cracks open

/ 6th day protestors

there is no
right or wrong

just the lies
we tell
to sleep at night

and the rules
we break
when no one's watching

/ hypocrisy

you can throw
your anger
into me

i'll carry it
like water does —
without losing my way

/ *skipping stones*

punch the wind
before you strike the stone

train the storm inside
before you swing
at the world

each breath
is a kata
each thought
a seed or a sword

discipline
does not begin
with muscle

but with a still mind
listening
before it moves

/ *shaolin*

you washed your hands
in the safety of daylight
but the moon
still knows the dirt beneath your nails

you locked every door
yet they come

/ can't you hear 'em knockin'

my heart
is a branch
and it breaks
each time
we fall again

/ *break-in-two*

i think now
is a good time
for jesus to come back —

the rivers
are choking
the forests
are burning

we are
too tired
to save ourselves

/ *second coming*

i wonder
if my bare feet
can outrun the wind

or if
like everything wild
it waits for me
to stop pretending

i'm not a part of it

/ *outrun the wind*

this country
throws around words
like fascism
        racism
           activism

as if they are

fashion trends
or
seasonal allergies

every ism
getting tossed around
with the warm sun

like they did something
like they bled for them

and the people
it actually hurts
are just outside
the evening news spotlights
still bleeding
still unheard —

but as you should know
you can't change a system
within a weekend
and a hashtag

/#

if you're gonna fight
do it with your whole breath
like it's the only thing
you were made for

some of us
got born in countries
where the bombs
don't fall on schools

we still make dinner
walk the dog
put our kids to bed

but we remind them
we're lucky
not better

and we say a quiet prayer
for the ones
who never made it home

/ *awareness*

bring back the mutineers
the ones who walked off
when the captain lost his mind

who said
this ship ain't going nowhere good
and jumped anyway

we called them crazy
but they were the only ones
who still remembered
how to swim

/ bring back the mutineers

do clowns scare us
as children
because we are still learning
that a painted smile
can lie

we do not yet know
that some people wear
laughter
the way others
wear armor

but we feel it
in our bones —
something isn't right
about the ones
who never stop
smiling

/fear the unknown

they say he fixes cars now
on the edge of town
no makeup
no mask
just oil on his hands
and a dog named balloon

kids still ask if he juggles
he says not anymore
but sometimes
he does
when no one's watching

/ *off-season*

the storm took the tent
before the show could start
ropes snapping
elephants confused
popcorn soggy on the grass

he just stood there
in the mud
face half-painted
waiting for someone to speak

/ it's okay to go

round

and

round

and

around

you go

/ tornado through a small town

a muskrat
has made its home
in the bones of ours
digging through concrete
like it was soft earth
reminding us
what's solid
never really is

/ shaking our foundation

if you dig
through the roots
of the american dream

plant seeds
for others
to harvest in spring

/ work for it

if you keep chasing
the setting sun
long enough —

one day
you'll forget the running
and it will rise
inside your eyes

/ set to rise

follow that tired line of smoke
into the mountain's ribs
she hasn't forgotten
how we carved her open
then walked away
like nothing happened

/ *bite out of an apple*

keep blowing dandelions
while you're running off

that yellow line
keeps growing behind you

like a highway
to a two-lane

it'll catch up sooner than you expect

/yellow lines

when i die
lay me down in the kudzu
no box
no stone
just green vines
pulling me back
the way it was always meant to be

/ let nature take me back

this water was clean
until the rich ran to the hills
and claimed the last drops for themselves

makes you think —
is there any water left
that hasn't been bought
or poisoned yet?

/pequoig

spit it out
you were never meant
to carry that fire
on your tongue

spit it out
words rot
when held too long

spit it out
wrap your tongue
around the thought
until it cracks

spit it out
bang your head
on the old stone wall
until the truth shakes loose

/poison mouth

help me remember
why we're running

were we chasing a dream
or fleeing the fear of staying

/ *was there a fire?*

the next messiah
is probably barefoot
walking the train tracks
singing to dandelions

/performant of no shoes

i shut my eyes
and everything glows

open them
and it's the same old darkness

turns out
even silver linings
have dead ends

/ [...]

poppies and peonies
as far as the eye can see
i used to cry
at beauty like that

now i barely blink
and wonder
what broke in me

/ *where is the color?*

the river
we thought would never end
has led us
to the sea
and no one told us
it could be louder
and softer
at the same time

/ behold

where are my golden
teeth and nails
i chewed through steel
worked with blistered hands
built dreams i can't afford

they told me
hard work was holy
but all i got
was a mouth full of dust

/ hard work pays off… some debts!

what happens
to the weight of the world
when no one's around
to pick it up for you

does it just sit there
waiting to crush you
or does it get lighter
when you're the only one holding it?

/ *weight of the world*

don't forget to take your pills
that's how mornings start now —
not with coffee,
but with plastic covered in plastic sealed inside plastic

you stare out the window,
watching people in cars drive by
wondering as it takes
six tries to open the "child-proof" bottle

the pills don't fix things,
but you take them —
because that's what we do

the world keeps spinning
like your legs don't ache,
like your thoughts don't skip

still —
you brush your teeth, feed the cat,
say thanks when the sun shows up
and bitch about it all day
until it puts you to sleep at night

/ don't forget to take your pills

the human race
running nowhere
in a maze
we built ourselves

/ *rat race*

the trees don't move
but they're always firs
to feel the storm coming,
first to catch fire when the summer gets too dry

they just stand there, doing nothing, saying nothing, and still
they get everything —

light, water, worship

no rush
no noise
just presence

meanwhile we're busy trying to matter, chasing finish lines
that keep moving, and they're already there —
rooted,
patient,
completely unbothered by the idea of progress

/ finish lines don't move on the forest floor

hard to balance
when you're somewhere else —
miles ahead
or
miles behind

either way
i'm breaking myself
just to pull you
from the smoke

/ *pulling you back*

if i passed you
under saturday's neon lights
would your eyes still know mine

/ *nashville*

how do you
drown the memories
when they are
the only breath
keeping your head
above water

/ *memory to drown*

this is home now

but the smells
in the wind

walking beside me

the town i left
settled into my skin

too deep to cut out

/ *air surely*

sunlight
hits the rust

flowers
turn to dust

/just part of the day

this wild horse
keeps dragging me
through thorns and riverbeds

i never held the reins
but blame myself
for every twist

the trail behind me
scattered with
wilted flowers

some days
i thought the horse knew the way

but i pulled back
and it vanished —

/gone with the wind

they stare longest
when you're sinking

like a wreck
off the shoulder of the road
their eyes
feed on the fire

give me the bad medicine
to hush the bones
this weather
has teeth
i better go where
the storm don't follow

/ caution flare

i saw him again
still as stone
perched midstream
like he's listening
for god in the current

and i knew
it was you
by how he didn't move

will you stay
like a prayer
tucked beneath pine needles

/ *blue heron*

thunder
sleeps beneath my ribs

a man
made of storms
waiting
for the rain

/ thunderman

they named a city
after a chief

but the world
should have been named
after you

you were the land
under the wind
a voice in the water —

now that you've left
the sky looks
a little confused

the birds ask where you've gone

and the sun still rises —

like a river
life moves
even the earth
when we ask it not to

/ *Chief Seattle*

~
rest in peace
~
Scott "Caveman" Renstrom

/ the end

Thank you for going on another journey with, *Runaway Clowns*.
Every poem in these pages was born from a restless heart—
one that refuses to stay silent. I hope you carry that same
fire with you, never afraid to question the masks we wear or
the world we live in.
If this book moved you, please consider leaving a review on
Amazon.
Your words help independent authors like me reach new
readers.
Keep learning from within.

Luke H. Snyder

www.ingramcontent.com/pod-product-compliance
Lightning Source LLC
Chambersburg PA
CBHW050902180626
46814CB00007B/2851